MY ART IS KILLING ME

MY ART IS KILLING ME

AND OTHER POEMS

AMBER DAWN

ARSENAL PULP PRESS
VANCOUVER

MY ART IS KILLING ME
Copyright © 2020 by Amber Dawn
Foreword copyright © 2020 by Doretta Lau

SECOND PRINTING: 2023

ARSENAL PULP PRESS
Suite 202 – 211 East Georgia St.
Vancouver, BC V6A 1Z6
Canada
arsenalpulp.com

The publisher gratefully acknowledges the support of the Canada Council for the Arts and the
British Columbia Arts Council for its publishing program, and the Government of Canada, and
the Government of British Columbia (through the Book Publishing Tax Credit Program), for
its publishing activities.

   Canada

Arsenal Pulp Press acknowledges the xʷməθkʷəy̓əm (Musqueam), Sḵwx̱wú7mesh (Squamish),
and səl̓ilwətaʔɬ (Tsleil-Waututh) Nations, custodians of the traditional, ancestral, and unceded
territories where our office is located. We pay respect to their histories, traditions, and
continuous living cultures and commit to accountability, respectful relations, and friendship.

Front cover design by Oliver McPartlin
Back cover and text design by Jazmin Welch
Cover and interior illustrations by Jaik Puppyteeth
Edited by Sachiko Murakami
Copy edited by Shirarose Wilensky
Proofread by Jaiden Dembo

Printed and bound in Canada

Library and Archives Canada Cataloguing in Publication:
Title: My art is killing me, and other poems / Amber Dawn.
Names: Dawn, Amber, 1974–author.
Identifiers: Canadiana (print) 20190217421 | Canadiana (ebook) 2019021743X |
ISBN 9781551527932 (softcover) | ISBN 9781551527949 (HTML)
Classification: LCC PS8607.A9598 M93 2020 | DDC C811/.6—dc23

for Vivek Shraya

CONTENT WARNING
AND AUTHOR STATEMENT

Further to the description found on the back cover, please know that the word "rape" occurs sixteen times throughout this book. Several of the poems explore how trauma—sexual violence, in particular—shapes story, both how stories are told and how stories are consumed by observers and audiences. Other themes include criminalized poverty, racism, cyber bullying and internet harassment, and mental health crises.

Early drafts of *My Art Is Killing Me* were composed amid conversations with other writers that occurred between late 2015 and early 2017—a time in which rape culture, racism and tokenism became even more pressing, to me, than the ongoing gravity and frequency of these topics. Plainly put: I seemed to be constantly debriefing dumpster fire bullshit occurring in the literary arts sector. Alongside of other responses and reactions, I turned to poetry to engage with some of the harms I've personally experienced or witnessed within the sector.

The "I" in a poem is never quite the I that we are. How could a narrative "I" stand in for all of our complexities and vastness? The "I" in a poem gets to be particular; the "I" is allowed to take a fixed and focused stance on the subject matter it is narrating. The "I" in *My Art Is Killing Me* is exhausted by expectations of courage and uniqueness and redemption. The "I" in these poems is angry and unscrewed and desperate.

The I that I am maintains the same purpose I put into action early in my writing career: I'm here for healing—mine, yours and, yes, maybe even healing the fallacious world around us.

I thank the survivor-identified readers who have asked that I include content warnings in my books.

CONTENTS

SPEAK YOUR TRUTH

DORETTA LAU

and in this
paid and weighted
space mostly women, increasingly
#diverse women, are told to write
what they know.

and in this
made and weighted
space I sign my memoir
with the message "speak your truth"

—Amber Dawn

Amber Dawn came into my life when I was at university, in an undergraduate poetry workshop. I still remember a poem of hers from that time that referred to the plant Queen Anne's lace. Her world seemed bigger than mine, her lexicon more robust. Even as a student she knew how to write about beauty, how to see what everyone else ignored, how to use poetic craft to create space for emotional engagement. I admired her powers of observation, her kindness, her curiosity. Back then, I never imagined that we would have the opportunity to publish and go on a journey together as writers beyond the classroom. Over the past two decades, I have seen Amber Dawn emerge as a mentor to artists across North America, a person who leads with empathy.

My Art Is Killing Me is imbued with the power of the conversations Amber Dawn has been having within the community. In these uncertain times, I have turned to her to discuss the state of writing and the relationships we have built around our work. She has advised me on how to handle difficult situations, taught me strategies to reduce suffering for myself and others. We've talked about how to address abuses of power and what to do after making a mistake. From her, I have learned how to be vulnerable and strong at the same time. This collection of poetry shines a light on one possible path to follow in our current reality, which I've come to think of as the worst timeline.

In order to receive what *My Art Is Killing Me* has to offer, we must feel safe in our bodies. Amber Dawn has taken care to provide safety so that we may choose to engage with these poems, which delve into her personal history to examine what has forged her as an artist. This book creates the expansiveness necessary for us to see and in turn to be seen. She never shies away from addressing what ails our communities, naming real world violence and intergenerational trauma in an act of witness.

In "Hollywood ending," a poem dissecting the American film industry's obsession with giving actresses awards for playing sex workers while pushing to make this form of labour illegal, stripping women who do this work of their personhood, Amber Dawn writes:

> I've begun to ask myself, how is it we fail
> to see nearby violence while we naively imagine distant violence.

Here, she lays it out so clearly: many of us live with the fantasy that our communities are free of violence, that these problems belong to other people. Many of us do not acknowledge what is happening in our classrooms and workplaces, nor do we have the vocabulary to express these experiences.

There is, however, a danger in being an artist so open on the page and vulnerable in the world. In "the stopped clock," Amber Dawn writes:

And besides, what's another bruise?
What's a bruise? What's a bruise? What's a blue moon bruise
to do but pull young blood to and fro like the tide? What's a bruise
but a testament to the sharp art of surrendering to time and place?

Must a psychic bruise be the cost to someone who does the work of being present, of "surrendering to time and place"? As I read the poem "Dear IncorrectName," I began to wonder why we expect artists to do our emotional labour for us. Is the violence of consumption inherent to experiencing art in our late-stage capitalist societies? For me, these questions are central to a reading of *My Art Is Killing Me,* which brings me back to a line in "Hollywood ending": "Tell me, who is being *consumed*?"

This collection makes it clear to me that art is for engagement, to bring people together in conversation. We are not meant to consume art, nor are we meant to consume creators, to ask that they suffer on our behalf. I believe we are compassionate enough to come to a book and to accept what the writer is offering us, and to not demand more. I want us to live in tenderness that is a choice, a display of vulnerability. I do not want us to be tender because we've had bruises inflicted upon us by the people around us.

What I'm trying to say is each time Amber Dawn publishes a book or edits an anthology, our communities and our literatures become more expansive. *My Art Is Killing Me and Other Poems* exemplifies her dedication to illuminating narratives that many people ignore, meeting discomfort with words rather than with silence. She is an artist who makes space for others to join in the conversation with our own stories. Her work across genres marries intellectual rigour, intricate craft, and emotional honesty to produce literature that is at once innovative and generous. As readers, when we finish reading an Amber Dawn book we feel clever, though she is the one who has done the critical thinking and shared the ideas in writing.

I keep going back to Amber Dawn's poem "outsider artist," which contains the lines: "And one more thing: I feel alone. I don't know who I can / trust at the academy or the author's table, myself included." Thanks to our friendship and her writing, I have never been alone. I trust Amber Dawn. I've sat at a table with her, seen the work that she does to encourage me, and so many other people, to speak my truth. Her words and her actions are a way forward. As I read *My Art Is Killing Me*, I recalled the somatic experiencing exercise where you tap every part of your body to welcome your soul back. Amber Dawn's precise words awaken us in this same way, guiding us back to our bodies, making us whole.

My mama: What? You're crying.
You wanna cry, eh? I'll give you something to cry about.

The rest of my life: You're writing confessional poetry, is that right?
Well, lah-de-dah, girl. I'll give you something to write poems about.

THE STOPPED CLOCK

I was costumed in a white tiger striped bodysuit when I found out
I'd been accepted into the graduate creative writing program
at the University of British Columbia. The bodysuit was one size
too small and my labia majora squeezed out from either side
of the gusset whenever I sat down.

I sat with the other sluts, most of whom I loved like stopped clock, around
a vinyl topped card table inside a corrugated steel barn in Huntsville, Alabama.
Our hosts brought warm tamales wrapped in tinfoil
and a one gallon glass jar of homemade moonshine.

From the moonshine I expected what I expect of every spirit
stronger than seventy proof. I expected a methanol spice akin to grappa
and I yearned for the zippered mountain road between Sulmona and Pacentro
along which I once vomited in the passenger side footwell of an Alfa Romeo.

The Italian word for vomit is *vomito*. Maybe it's nostalgia, but *vomito* sounds
so cute. Like something you could name a small pet.

Moonshine flint behind my ears.
My cell phone lit with a 604 area code.

The admission secretary's voice high and bright despite
her calling from four thousand plus kilometres away.
She said *I'm so happy for you*
and *your acceptance letter is in the mail*
and *you should apply for a scholarship.*

Did the secretary know my livelihood was pussy tap?
It's likely the entire selections committee knew.
My writing sample rough packed
with so many poems about men's billfolds. Ass
ass ass cash and allusion: my nascent body of work.

Our MC, Annie the Bandit, announced my big news to the audience. Their clanging
applause surprised me. It shouldn't have, because a whore that goes to college
is adorable. Live-nude-crook to hit-the-books is a narrative string
any fella can feel good about tucking a fiver into.

The woozy decked stage caught my stiletto. The sound of my knees
pounding plywood barely audible against the sonic boom of burlesque.

And besides, what's another bruise?
What's a bruise? What's a bruise? What's a blue moon bruise
to do but pull young blood to and fro like the tide? What's a bruise
but a testament to the sharp art of surrendering to time and place?

And how I surrendered to the stage, quit the clamour
of spectator expectancy, the scream pitched ringing in the round.

I bowed down to ageless filth and glitter and leaked fluid, O striptease stage
O hallowed ground. I prayed to the ghosts of every hustler who's turned rock
ballads into rent, grind into gold. Face downed belly rolled until I met god
or a staph infection. Same difference.

This is definitely nostalgia talking. Don't let me (and my tilt towards glorification) fool you.

The truth is I uprighted myself and finished my set just like any other night.

The one concrete detail I recall about the mother, who presented me
with her virgin teenage son that night in the barn, was her pearls.

                                                                            Nacreous
is the adjective that describes the specific lustre of a pearl. Her pearls
had flawless nacre. Not like the poor flaking strand
passed down to me by my nonna
and we were in Alabama.

The mother in pearls was interested
in buying sex for her teenage son.

He must become a man before going off to college.
She was certain it was his virginity that hindered him
from the kingdom and the power of predestined manhood.

What she was unsure of
was how much I should
be paid for my service.

I sometimes wonder (though do not care in the slightest) if pity was the reason I was accepted into the creative writing program at the University of British Columbia. Wild card candidate, long odds.

An anagram for "creative writing" is "tragic interview"

I would have to veer into fantasy to continue the story
about Alabama. There is nothing I remember
about the virgin teenage son.

To write what little appears on this page, I've superimposed the Geek
from the 1984 film *Sixteen Candles* and alternatively Brian
from *The Breakfast Club*. A John Hughes constructed outcast
crying over thwarted masculinity and a tenuous ability
to subjugate teenaged women's bodies.

I grew up with movies that taught me the meek
shall inherit the prom. Or the Geek shall inherit
access to a blackout drunk cheerleader.

But life rarely mimics a Hollywood ending.
Or does it? One sure thing: sex
work isn't going anywhere.

I paid tuition, yes absolutely, and also I spent my pussy tap money travelling. In Pacentro, I saw the 553rd *Corsa degli Zingari*. In the village dialect, *zingari* describes those who are barefoot.

Barefoot young men walk the mule trail up Mount Morrone

    past malnourished stray dogs that haunt the village cemetery, past

      their ancestors resting in the high walls, past

        cicadas keening in the warped heat. Higher still, past

          stone huts where shepherds have slept since time immemorial, past

            dregs of scorched *secondo dopoguerra* earth, past

              brown bear and antelope tracks, past

                prayer caves, past

                  consecrated bedrock, past unmarked graves.

                    For the past five and a half centuries barefoot young men

                      have waited at the top of Morrone rock

                        for the starting bell to echo through Peligna Valley.

The ringing bell made me cry for reasons I still do not understand.

I lined up with the other onlookers and watched barefoot young men race
to the finish line at the feet of the Virgin Mary. Bloody footprints on the church floor

a rite of passage.

Those who reached the Virgin became good men, heroes
spread in a dusty huddle before the altar. The Virgin of Loreto (or the Virgin
in this particular church) was pale blue gold and haloed in the kind
of electric lights that bring to mind an old Hollywood dressing room.

Filmdom vanity, ersatz divinities, I'm all in. And because I've seen every Fellini film, I
too kissed the Virgin's stone toes and prayed. The villagers called me

stonata figlia   it means something
like the confused daughter, the girl   out
of step   with the rest, but still   space
was made for my queer body
to kneel down and pray.

For as long as I can remember I've been afraid. Afraid of the pitiful narrations my body has been inscribed into, and now that I've refashioned this memory into a poem I choose not to show myself praying the rosary psalms or any grace I learned as a girl.

I prayed *please*

I don't want to be
afraid anymore.

I'll do anything, please

Ho paura.
Paura lasciami.

Please.

Unafraid.
Please.

You (literally you) are reading queer and desperate poetry, and so
I already love you like a stopped clock, but if you're wondering
whether or not I took that Alabamian mother's money
to fuck her virgin son then you too better

kneel down and pray.

The other sluts dropped me, and my bag
full of animal print lingerie and the small grimy bills I hustled
in the South, at O'Hare airport in Chicago. They kept touring
the Midwest, Milwaukee, maybe Minneapolis and eventually
into the lonesome sphere of memory. (These days, if I can't find
an old friend through Google I assume they are dead.)

I flew back to Vancouver to attend the University
of British Columbia, where more than one professor warned me
not to confuse creative writing with therapy.

HOLLYWOOD ENDING

Jack Nicholson (playing an alcoholic with no fixed address): *Oh, come on.*
At least you got to sing a song.

Meryl Streep (playing a sex worker): *Yeah, I did. I sang*
while Sandra was dying over there.

                                        —*Ironweed* | drama | Rated R | 1987

Filmdom vanity, ersatz divinities. By the year 2015, twenty five actresses
had received Academy Award nominations for playing sex workers onscreen.

In 2015, over twenty five actresses signed a letter opposing human rights
organization Amnesty International's proposed policy to decriminalize sex work.

(There is a sizable overlap
between these two celebrity sets.)

       Winner Elizabeth Taylor | *Butterfield 8* | Best Actress
       in a Leading Role

       Winner Anne Hathaway | *Les Misérables* | Best Actress
       in a Supporting Role

       Nominee Meryl Streep | *Ironweed* | Best Actress
       in a Leading Role

On why she didn't join other actresses in speaking up again rapist and predator Harvey Weinstein, Meryl Streep said *I wasn't deliberately silent. I didn't know this was happening.*

The letter Meryl Streep signed opposing decriminalization reads *should Amnesty vote to support the decriminalization of* ["]*pimping brothel owning and sex buying*["]*, it will in effect support a system of* ["]***gender apartheid***["]*, in which one category of women may gain protection from sexual violence ... while another category of women ... are instead set apart for consumption by men ...*

Amnesty's reputation in upholding human rights ... would be severely and irreparably tarnished if it adopts a policy that [*decriminalizes sex work*]*.*

Oh double dealing feminism. Oh slut scapegoating—I can't.
And I can't ask this poem to explain the error of conflating sex work
with trafficking either. Catch that education elsewhere.

I have cumulative considerations now, adjacent thoughts: Streep *didn't know* actresses
were being raped by a Hollywood mogul she'd worked closely with for years, though
she claims to know, and is willing to speak for, a *category of women*—meaning sex
workers—whom she believes are being *consumed by men*.

Another consideration, an epitomist thought: To fail to see, or to intentionally overlook
sexual violence happening in close proximity—perpetual sexual violence in an industry
that makes a select few into millionaires, like Streep, whose net worth is estimated
at $90 million, to overlook this close and perpetual and profitable sexual violence
while
making large, as in globally fucking large, assumptions and would be decisions
about the sexual violence happening to unseen and stigmatized sex workers
is

is

is   is

is, uhm   is
is what, for pity's sake

is   is

is what

?

What would you (literally you) call this anomaly, where Streep (in this poem Streep

now presents as a composite, a widespread viewpoint, got it?) doesn't see

the sexual violence happening to colleagues right beside her

while

she imagines sexual violence happening to truly invisibilized

workers around the world, and that she is an authority

on ending this sexual violence, as she imagines it?

Tell me, who is being *consumed*?

Nominee Sophia Loren | *Matrimonio all'italiana* | Best Actress
in a Leading Role

Winner Mira Sorvino | *Mighty Aphrodite* | Best Actress
in a Supporting Role

Winner Jane Fonda | *Klute* | Best Actress
in a Leading Role

In 1996, Oscar ceremony host Whoopi Goldberg noted that three of the ten actresses
nominated that year had played the part of sex workers. Elisabeth Shue for *Leaving
Las Vegas*, Sharon Stone for *Casino*, and Mira Sorvino.

> In 1996, I turned outdoor low rent full service sex, and I watched
> the Oscars at a basement translady and leatherdyke bar: a beautiful
> bent heaven that I thought would last forever
> but now I've veered into queer grit again.
> As I do.

After her big win for starring in a Woody Allen film, Sorvino became a mighty
anti trafficking advocate. She even played the part of a Russian American cop
who saves women across Eastern Europe from the "hellish existence
of brutality and prostitution" (show's synopsis quoted) in a miniseries called *Human
Trafficking*. In interviews, Sorvino has stated, many times, that prostitution
breeds sex trafficking.

In 1971, Jane Fonda won her first Oscar for her role as Bree Daniels, a sex worker
and since, Fonda stated, many times, that sex work should never be legalized.

I think about this a lot—
what it means to launch an illustrious career playing
the part of someone you believe is singularly synonymous
with violence and exploitation.

What it means to play the part
of someone you believe should not legally exist.

Who is being consumed?
What is being consumed?

Besides being a popular role for actresses, sex workers are one
of the most researched and reported on populations in the world.

Many of these reports can quantify how many times the sex workers, who were
interviewed, were raped and, with some inference, what the likelihood of rape
is among populations of sex workers.

I was interviewed by a researcher who asked me these very questions:

Have you ever been raped?   *By a client?*   *How many times?*

Between 1 and 3 times?
More than 5 times?
More than 10?

Where you ever raped
multiple times
by the same client?

Have you ever reported
a rape?

For my story, I was paid in public transit tickets
and a ten dollar gift card for the local pharmacy.

This early lesson about story taught me that my own personal narrative is very cheap.

There are **no** reports on how many times sex workers have prevented rape.

There are almost **no** reports on how we keenly see present and potential sexual violence around us and how frequently we practise violence intervention. **No** reports surveying how common it is for sex workers to speak up about predatory men. **No** reports that quantify how our readiness to speak up and to intervene has reduced sexual violence in our industries. **No** reports that show sex workers' efforts and effectiveness in tangibly supporting rape survivors in healing (as opposed to obsessing over the reputations of predatory men as is common in Hollywood, literary publishing and academia). **No** reports that capture the practical applications of anti violence strategies   sex workers have employed   for an eternity.

This anti violence wisdom falls outside
of institutional and Hollywood imagination.

I am eleven years retired from full service sex work and eight
years retired from any form of sex work whatsoever.

When I had cock in my mouth I never pictured Hollywood endings.
(Though, sometimes, I did loop lines of poetry in my mind.)

Only now do I have the privilege to consider the implications of famous
rich white women wannabe rescuing poor, mostly racialized and migrant
and invisibilized women as a status boosting hobby.

Only now have I begun to wonder why
Hollywood actresses are so hot damn desperate
to draw distinctions between themselves and sex workers.

I've begun to ask myself, how is it we fail to see
nearby violence while we naively imagine distant violence?

I have cumulative considerations, adjacent thoughts that I will surely flip
and flip and flip and flip and flip throughout this book and forever.
How are we imagining the lives of others?

What are we failing to see? What vulnerability, yes, and also what agency and what
resiliency are we overlooking? What do we gain from the imagined or quantifiable
stories of others? How does story, and our interpretations of it, determine
who we blame and who we protect? How does story decide what we
subjugate and what we celebrate? Think about it, sex work is both
invisible and it is a mirror. Hold it up.
Don't think this isn't about you.

Tell me, who is being *consumed*?

Mira Sorvino (playing a sex worker): *And so there I am on the first day, on the set, and
there's this guy fucking me from behind, right, and there's these two huge guys dressed like
cops in my mouth at the same time and I remember thinking to myself, "I like acting."*

—*Mighty Aphrodite* | comedy | Rated R |1995

AN APPLE, OR *HAUNTED*

Hold a winesap apple to your brow and think of the worst
possible outcome. Or has the worst already happened?

How do you define cataclysm? Does your ruin have
an aroma, a taste? Can you imagine ruin in your mouth?

Does ruin conjure a colour palette? A visual pattern?
Project ruin's image through the apple. Ask the apple to see
what you see, sense what you sense, to be wounded with you.

Cut the wounded fruit in half with a black handled knife
if you own one. Eat the half that falls to your right.

A winesap will honey your nose and sop your tongue.
Let blush and sweetness in. Bury the left half in your garden.

I was a knuckle drunk tattooed queer runaway since I was sixteen but it wasn't until age thirty seven when I announced my engagement that my nonno disowned me.

His scribbled two sentence castoff
reminded me that he was illiterate

"hell" and "dead"
spelled correctly

then there was
"emooral"

e   m   o   o   r   a   l

in context: "your emooral life"
a small tear between "o"s where his pen

heavily retraced the vowels
like an infinity symbol

I'd like to say something true and complete about compassion.

All my abusers are survivors after all.
Nonno   no different

My ma told me he died in a trailer so
poverty gnawed she could see the sky
through the aluminum walls.

By and by my mind coupled the pen torn disownment letter with the holes in his trailer. Together these images made the most dreamy grief imaginable. Is this compassion? When the mind processes trauma through metaphor is it compassion?

Or it this only   the beginning of another
publish ready piece for my body-of-work?

When the mind processes trauma through metaphor it's pretty easy
to write a fantasy novel. My first book was a fantasy novel
and also my MFA thesis. I doubt I would have graduated without fantasy.

I mean, what survivor can hold up their unbroken   reality
in the academy? Fantasy is strategy. Tunnel light. It's the genre
that would allow me to pen *The End*.

I had this romantic idea that I'd finish the last draft of my thesis
in my hometown where white tailed deer sway so close like danger
is just something I made up in my head. Maybe I'd make peace with
my ma (again), I thought, only she refused to let me stay in her
spare room, claiming her third husband was a homophobe
their new marriage too delicate for me and my fantasy
novel tramp their narrow bungalow.

      Returning to Vancouver seemed depressing.
    My thesis advisor was on extended sick leave
  and my partner was about to queer divorce me
and besides the hero in my fantasy novel can't
remember the name she was given at birth.
That's the central conflict: the hero's lost
track of her past, she doesn't belong
anywhere, and so going back
to my hometown to finish
writing felt like a fit
like a creative fit
you know? So I
moved into
a cheap
rental
and
dug
in.

Set a timer for one minute. Close your eyes
and pay attention to what you smell and hear
to what you feel and think.

Think about anything
except an apple.

Don't think about an apple.
Not skin or juice. Not seed or core.

Better still, wipe the colour red
from your mind altogether.

If you think about an apple, reset the timer
as many times as it takes.

The task is to go one minute
without thinking about an apple.

The mind processes trauma through metaphor.

I last saw my nonno
while writing my thesis in that cheap rental in my hometown. He flew from Miami
to Buffalo, then rented a car for the backwoods drive. Maybe he thought he would
make peace with my ma (again) too. She sounded trouble bumped on the phone—
He stays with you. Not with me, you. He's too old to make it up a flight of stairs.
Sleep upstairs and he won't be able to get to you.

In my family we love each other from 100 yards away, a restraining
order kind of love. And I pitied him, this man who would never
tell me where exactly he was born, who wouldn't name
his first daughter and so ma's birth certificate
reads *Coppola, girl*. This man who
forever walked with a cane
and could lift me up
by my throat.

I made him spaghetti.
What else could I do?

When he ran his pinky along
the empty dinner plate for one last taste of primavera sauce
I decided to make him a character. Not an antagonist
(there are no villains in any of my books) more so
a trope from Joseph Campbell's monomyth
a supporting character to help my lost hero
through the Night Sea Voyage chapter.

A hermit living in supernatural darkness
sustained by the memories
of sentimental yesterday
and an unusually high
tolerance for
silence.

Right okay, theory [lite]

the Night Sea Voyage same same

Belly of the Whale same same, Return

to the Womb all but same, the Hermit card

from the tarot deck yeah same, River Styx not

quite same same, the Unspeakable Void same and same

I've got nothing to say about Carl Jung and the unconscious

but knock yourself out and same same, and while I'm at it same

difference to every single therapeutic survivor themed workbook I ever

half completed, not far from same as step four in the Alcoholics Anonymous

Big Book ("to make a searching and fearless moral inventory of ourselves")

The questions are as good as same:

How does your character (you) deal with fear?

Will your character (you) traverse the terrifying unknown?

Who does your character (you) depend on?

And are they (you) now willing to go it alone?

What notions of self must your character (you) renounce?

What do they (you) need to learn about their true name?

And maybe:

What desires is your character (you)
trying to conceal, control or express?

How will these desires take shape?

Do they (you) have protective talismans (coping skills)
in place before the journey of desires begins?

Ultimately:

Will you (your character) go to that deep deep lonely place that uncertain
place that guarded guarded inside place that *you have no power here, child*
that desperate place that *how hungry are you? and what will you do*
for food? that place where the stomach eats itself where the tongue
tastes strange blood that choke and retch place that humiliated
empty handed place where there are fewer than zero
guarantees that what you see and what you learn
will make you any more capable
of existing in the larger world
anyway   but ultimately
your unique truth must
mean something, right?

Will you complete this task?

The hero in my novel fulfills her Night Sea Voyage relatively unscathed.
The truth is I could never, and will never, punish
my protagonists. High stakes conflict feels too much like

         self harm.

       Have I mentioned that I love writing fantasy?
        Gaga for that arc, I am. Pyramid my life!

    Have I mentioned that the first and only literary agent to read
my fantasy novel said she was surprised none of my characters died.
She expected more high stakes conflict in a book about sex workers.

I made my hero and the hermit share a slice of apple pie
before they part ways. No guff, the Night Sea chapter acts
as a substitute goodbye, an earth salt earnest goodbye
that Nonno and I would never
realize in real time.

When the mind processes trauma through metaphor, what does closure look like?

Okay, all reverie aside, I'm so suspicious of "closure" or any psychology that gives grief finality. Closure seems too neat and white. Closure is sold in a neat white-on-white minimalist boutique were the widely spaced products have no visible price tags. Closure is like the conspicuous consumption of real life.

Maybe the highest stakes in my first book, also my MFA thesis, are found in the final two words: *The End.*

After Nonno passed Ma wanted to heart to heart—*He was
an awful drunk. You're lucky you never saw him at his worst.*

She arts-and-crafts collaged her original birth
certificate, *Coppola, girl*. Blessed it with gold
and red glitter. She loves sparkle.
And red is her favourite colour.

And all of us are telling a story on the surface
of another story.
                    Even if that story is made
from Elmer's® Classic Glitter Glue.

I'm not fluent in my nonno's language, but I know
la mela stregata means the poison apple. Or more
literal, *the bewitched apple.*   Or *haunted.*

Earth   Water   Fire   Air and   the Void
each apple has a five pointed star hidden within.

All fine and unknown things and, yes
also how the mind processes trauma

through metaphor
journey
fantasy
poetry
belly
knell
call
spark
dark
din

din
dark
spark
call
knell
belly
poetry
fantasy
journey
and metaphor

I'd still like to say something about compassion.

HOW HARD FEELS

Through a filmy single paned window I see
one of my TAs cross the campus lawn. Early morning
she cuts a path in the damp grass. All I've learned
about her so far is that she cares deeply for the needed weave
of coastal biodiversity and that she loves old movies.

The tenured professor
sprints behind
briefcase   camel coat   I can't hear
the words he calls out   only
that she stops when his mouth moves

He reaches for her shoulder
do I see circular touch
hairsweep fingerdance   mere seconds
trap flash   they fall out   of the window's frame
before I can   lift myself from my desk

                                        everywhere there is a man

It is exaggeration to call the desk "mine"
It's a satellite desk, a workspace shared by adjunct instructors
in the creative writing program at the University of British Columbia.
Still, I've asserted myself by pinning two personal
portraits to the shared corkboard:

The first portrait: a national newspaper interview
for which (against my better judgment) I posed
beside a chain link fence along a track I call blow job alley. The headline
reads "Sex trade worker turns poet—and gives back with a frank memoir"

                                        everywhere there is a man

The second: a pen and ink illustration of my head with the body
of a mermaid, drawn by an undergrad on the last day
of my poetry workshop. Around the me-mermaid bull kelp
and eelgrass spins into the words "speak your truth"

"speak your truth" is how I sign my memoir
whenever I'm asked for an autograph

Years before, the tenured professor reaches
for my thigh under a long Formica table while my short story
about pig farms is being discussed in his class.

                                                    everywhere there is a man

Again my thigh in his office
circular touch   righthand blur between
counsellor and lech as he tells me *I know*
it's hard but push push push yourself.
You can write yes talent talent yes talent if
you push push push yourself. I can see you
going all the way.

                                                    everywhere there is a man

                                        everywhere there is a man

a man who knows it's hard
a man with an office door

                                        everywhere there is a man

he spoons wise guidance so familiar
with what ought to be said and when

                                        everywhere there is a man

    with a running tab at the bar
    with a car parked right outside

                                        everywhere there is a man

    who waxes past or future favour
    he will make introductions if he can

                                        everywhere there is a man

        with an agent who might be just
        might be looking for new voices

                        everywhere there is a man

                    everywhere there is a man
                    everywhere there is a man

I began my memoir at university. I thought if I was
going to break the book world it would be by writing
an outsider memoir. Then Sheila went missing
and Shelby was found

dead in a shopping cart
behind a laundromat

and I turned
decidedly
to fiction

                                        everywhere there is a man
                                        everywhere there is a man
                                        everywhere there is a man
                                        everywhere there is a man
                                        everywhere there is a man

a man who knows it's hard

who remembers being a nobody himself back when

humble start don't say he was handed a damn thing

                                        everywhere there is a man

who has rolled up his sleeves pulled socks cut teeth tooth and nail hammer

and the anvil nosed the grindstone made headway measured that extra mile

                        everywhere there is a man

so red hot for taxonomy for hashtags not all men

pudwacking hot for the adage my sword is my pen

                        everywhere there is a man
                        everywhere there is a man

When
I first abandoned my memoir the tenured professor
said he was disappointed. He asked *Are you afraid*
that after you write down everything that happened

you will no longer be lovable?

Eighteen years later and still this troubles me. For a long
time I questioned why   the fuck   would he say that?

Eventually it was his particular usage of *afraid*
and *lovable* that became utterly unfathomable.

afraid
and lovable

afraid
and lovable

The meaning of these words
lost somewhere between
his gender and mine.

                                        everywhere there is a man

he speaks a cryptic tongue and calls it universal
a language he is willing to teach his favourite pupils

                    everywhere there is a man

he knows how it feels how rule feels how words feel how hard feels
how voice feels how deals feel he knows how hard feels he knows hard
he gets it and after everything he's done

                              everywhere there is a man

a thank you is the very least credit due
recognition after everything he's done
after everything he's done

                                        everywhere there is a man

                                        everywhere there is a man

                                        everywhere there is a man

                                        everywhere there is a man
                                        everywhere there is a man
                                        everywhere there is a man

Everywhere there is a woman   queer or fury or holding her beloved body
however she can everywhere there is a woman working her masked craft
invisible labour ungraspable praxis her voice shivering out a frequency
only other women can hear her unsung opera her nixed lexicon censored
origin stories publicly mocked creation myths her hands quick quick so quick
undetectable a slight a secret she never has to reveal   other women already know
the shape of a veiled monument   already follow her pen and ink abstracts
recognize the portraiture the cut paper silhouette her undersold landscapes
remaindered biography her biblioruin already follow the end and footnotes
already hears the brutal anaphora be harassed see harassment
be**harassed**see**harassment** be**harassed**see**harassment** oh violent grandatio
other women already spin that loop already co positioned below the surface
everywhere there is a woman shaping and reshaping and reshaping the deep
lower than thermocline that sunless room of her own underwater spinning
bull kelp and eelgrass into words that only other women will ever look for

                                                    "speak your truth"

                                        everywhere there is a man

                                        everywhere there is a man

                                        everywhere there is a man

STREGHERIA INSTRUCTIONAL #1

For a spell I directed my fear at the waning moon. She's the oldest woman
around and she knows to flinch left from a punch.

Do women learn how to take punches from the moon?
Our crises are as recurrent as the lunar cycle, true
though far less visible than a halo.

For the *fuck you moon* spell I allowed myself
thirteen and a half nights each month to tell
the waning moon   fuck it

fuck this fuck me fuck him fuck him

fuck her fuck pain fuck poor decisions

fuck indecision fuck power fuck blame

fuck forgiveness fuck powerlessness fuck

fuck anger fuck pretending not to be angry

fuck silence fuck lateral violence fuck

fuck this noise

fuck this noise

fuck this noise

and fuck him

and fuck

this noise

and fuck

me

When the moon disappeared, I took a breath.

Reset. Reflect.

The new moon is a time to ask for guidance.

FOUNTAINHEAD

Sure, I've tossed three pennies over my left shoulder into Trevi
Fountain in Rome, but the mermaid fountain in Piazza Sannazaro
Napoli is my favourite. Napoli is a city of mermaids. I lost count

of mermaids. Two tailed and bathing in cracked frescoes. Marble
reliefs carved into arched doorways. Mermaid faces on old coins.
I almost bought myself a Tears of Parthenope necklace. A gold

chain hung with two blue teardrop shaped Swarovski crystals.
Parthenope and her sisters swam (or flew, myth shows sirens as half
bird or half fish. Either femme beast works) to Ulysses's ship to curse

him with their song, but Ulysses tied himself to the mast, stopped
his ears with wax and withstood. The entire crew of men survived
simply by not listening, so the story goes and goes. The defeated

mermaids wept at their failure and salt water filled the Bay of Naples.
Parthenope died from the shame and was swept ashore. Her blonde hair
turned to sand and her body, stone. A beach I myself have walked along.

I audibly sobbed before the gorgeous baroque blood of Artemisia
Gentileschi's famous *Judith Slaying Holofernes*, on permanent
display at the Uffizi. A man my father's age asked me nine

times to leave the gallery with him. One of the only Italian
phrases I know so well that my subconscious has spoken it
back to me in dreams is *lasciami stare*. It means leave me alone.

I drank too much at the strip club in Pescara, Abruzzo as a topless dancer
listed the times homophobia nearly killed her. I understood her perfectly
when she asked what Canada is like. Is there *libertà per lesbi* in Canada?

I furiously recorded the words that I misunderstood in a notebook
as if I might one day retroactively follow meaning. I couldn't call
upon language fast enough to console her in real time. I couldn't say

fuck this shit, I'm so sorry or *chin up, tits out, you know* or *you
deserve better, femme.* I've come to associate speaking half a language
or less than half, a tender handful of comprehension, with being

a survivor of sexual violence. My body has breath and spasm where it
should have words. My body can picture ease and desire, but is forever
learning how to say what it wants. I spent a humble lifetime looking for

others who too labour to live inside their skin My kink is to loudly love those
who've been told to keep quiet. Erotic boom. I want outlaster love. Against-
all-odds love. I, finally, want myself, and I want slick fluency in this desire.

While in Napoli I wrongly read a museum label to say that Parthenope
wished to marry Circe the sorceress. I read queer determination, and imagine
how that ancestral beach might feel if my mistranslation was an origin story.

Imagine if the grounds we walk were built from queer love? What song would our queer scion sing six thousand years from now? What shape would story take? If our bodies were safe and fluid loose, waxy and loud

and fluent in a *madrelingua,* in a kin spit, in the looped vernaculars we have long deserved, then imagine what words we'd know so well that even our subconscious could speak this love back to us in a dream.

BOOTHEEL

I launched my memoir in a classroom at the University of British Columbia
not the creative writing classroom where my perfect bound thesis is shelved.

It was a glass walled hall where human relationships are studied.
The tenured professor was there, seated in the back row beside his TA.

It was late March and raining. The coffee urn and free pastries made me
think of AA meetings. I told the audience the earliest missing women's

posters appeared in Vancouver's Downtown Eastside in 1998. I told them
that it was a trick, not the police, who designed and distributed those posters.

I told them in 1998 I lived at 350 Carrall Street across from Pigeon Park
and the Vancouver Co-op Radio station and I saw those posters every day.

I told them there was still a basement dyke bar two blocks down
with neon mud flap girls to mark the entrance. Sometimes a bunch

of us from Monday night's women survivors of sexual assault support
group would go there to drink vodka sevens without any men around.

Maybe I can trace my early memoir writing back to that support group.
The leader suggested we write down the location of where we were raped.

Just the location, not our rapists' names, not the unspeakable details.
I wrote *big rig sleeper gas station parking lot*. At the end of the exercise

the leader had us tear up the paper, scatter the shreds on the linoleum floor
and stomp around. I worried a shred from another women's rape location

would get stuck to my boot. I'd been made afraid of survivors' stories
mine especially. Violence is one sharp thing, how we speak about it

and how we listen is another. I didn't disclose to the other women
from the support group that I was raped by a bad date. I was by far

the youngest and was nicknamed little sister. *You're okay, little sister*
you're going to be okay—this from the mouths of women my ma's age

loosened a hard tangle in me but not loose enough to admit that I
turned street dates for cruelly low pay. What if they thought I deserved it?

Survival has always been about omitting parts of the story
about speaking only permissible words in permissible situations.

Maybe it was pervasive omission that prompted me to enroll in a poetry workshop
in 1998. I fixate on beginnings as if clinching a starting point will allow me to begin

all over again. I told the audience that there used to be coyotes on campus
and their skinny silhouettes made me homesick. All this preamble before

I even cracked my memoir's spine. When I did read, I traced my index finger
along the page as if I would lose my place. It wasn't my debut, I knew how to hold

a microphone, but the word "memoir" in bold font beside my cover photo
made me nervous. Baby pink lipstick was trending and I noticed the TA and I

both wore the same shade of *it's a girl*. At the book signing table she hugged
the kind of hug I now recognize as wounded affinity. No one ever touched me

when I read from my first book—a fantasy novel. She was teaching me
something, or rather, she was confirming what I already suspected

that memoir would have me inhabit a kind of paradoxical body:
evident and abstract body, present and detached body, a body

that invites readers to wrap their arms around so that they might embrace
themselves. And, too, she was reminding me that I only ever wanted to write

for other survivors. The tenured professor suggested I visit his office
to discuss my career. How unalike his handshake was from the TA's hug.

I passed him his signed copy and to this day I wince at how many abusers have touched
memoir. My handled story. Our handled stories. I barely remember the trick who ashed

his cigarette in my hair as I was performing a $40 blow job, but at night I beg myself
to quit thinking about the tenured professor's office and about my career. At night

I wrap my arms around my paradoxical body so that I might, finally, embrace myself.

At a later time, a friend tells
me *the tenured professor*
blurbed my first book
his backing quote in print
one thousand times on her
inaugural text before his
name became tantamount
to sexual misconduct.

At a lateral time, the tenured professor's headshot
batters my mentions. I fear his smug mug shown
so often beside the word *allegations* is
an intentional silencing tactic.

I see three women holding hands in the front row of a panel
discussion where I'm speaking on the topic of underrepresentation
and resilience in literature. I am four thousand miles and ten years apart
from my thesis at the University of British Columbia and I understand
these three women are creative writing students and are traumatized.
Did you hear about the tenured professor? they ask during the question
and answer period. *How did you survive the tenured professor?*
How do we survive the tenured professor?

At an illimitable time, the creative writing MFA
student body is mostly women

and if the academy more than lip serves
their admissions policy, #diverse women.

And tenured professors are over-
whelmingly men

and white
and norm

and in this
paid and weighted
space mostly women, increasingly
#diverse women, are told to write
what they know.

and in this
made and weighted
space I sign my memoir
with the message "speak your truth"

       "speak your truth"
an easy acclamation, not invalid, but easy
easy easy easy easy   except speaking
your truth heels such heavy consequence.

The tenured professor is a composite character, a nonfiction
writing device (a device that was taught to me by
the tenured professor) where several real life individuals
who perform the same actions are represented by an amalgam
for the sake of reader comprehension, to streamline the narrative.

But you (literally you) are reading queer and desperate poetry
so may I assume you too have never been afforded
an uncomplicated story? Does streamlining
imply a certain luxury
that is not yours?

What you get is the uncertain the cyclical the lateral the latterly the eventual
the inevitable the ceaseless the compounded the concurrent the terminal
the tactical and the systemic? Is that about right?

Beside I can't afford another statement. Who can afford another statement?
libel and slander lawsuit damages damages damages filed in court file under
open letter under op-ed reputation reputation men men the accused men gag
Who gets to name names?

I can't bring myself to write
his name their names the tenured professors the media men
the editors the best selling authors the artistic directors
the false mentors the agents the handshake artists
the abusers.

I can't write names, not the un-
speakable details either, but you
follow.   You already know.

OUTSIDER ARTIST

A young man in a team jersey waits for me at the back
of the lecture hall. We just wrapped our penultimate

introduction to craft class and I prepare to be asked
for an extension, calculating assignment deadlines

and marking time in my mind as I come up the low
pile carpeted stairs. End of term thrashes students

the entire campus hard swollen. I can give him
an extra three days, or five. The projectors whir

as they power down, screens behind me blink black.
I turn back to see four hundred empty swivel chairs

and become suddenly cognizant of my gait.
Do I appear damaged to him, like a woman

who's had her pelvis fractured? (I am a woman
who's had her pelvis fractured.) Smile. Stay open

I remind myself, stay generous. *I heard that you used
to* his slow motion mouth *some guys from the team*

were talking he stands between me *we looked you up
online* and the exit. I should say no *naked photo* assert

a student/professor boundary *porno* redirect him. My TA
motions in the periphery. *Women's intuition*, she tells me

as she walks me back to my office. She got a weird feeling.
Afterward I automate through conversations with counselling

services, academic advising, the director of the equity
office. I decline to speak with the team coach directly.

When I recount what happened to the equity director
I wonder what if she thinks I deserve it? What if she

is the type of feminist who romances a rarefied anti-
violence movement, if only sex workers (and trans

women) would drop from sight? Addressing rape culture on
campus is laborious enough without a femme presenting

ex hooker in the lecture hall. Calm down, I caution myself.
I censor the word *pornography*, even though *porn* is what

the young man said, that is, his team
found my naked body on the internet.

Moving forward: campus security escorts me to and from
my last class, compulsory counselling for the young man.

Only alone with my wife at our dinner table do I cry
about how stupid I am for believing I could teach

a whole term without being sexually harassed, without
my history or identity wrung. How many times must I

be hard taught the same lesson: disclosure is a great-
er risk to me than to the men whose violence I speak to.

This is true for all women. The shame of back-
sliding into psychic poverty, associative injury

the familiar pull and knot of pain that makes
talking to the equity director the same as talking

to police offers, social workers, the intake nurse
at the short term treatment centre years ago, so-

called power holders who required my story to be
worded a specific way before support was granted

or not. The whiteness that tipped me the script
and the whiteness that ensured I was heard

my whiteness that believes I deserve to tell my survivor's
story and one day be paid for such damn courage, be shown

the stage the lectern the interview the short list the ceremony.
The young man in a team jersey calls all this bone close again.

And one more thing: I feel alone. I don't know who I can
trust at the academy or the author's table, myself included.

Who do I confide in about pain when pain is my praxis
and best performance? I have watched pavement dry

sponge my blood, my attacker left me for dead and gone, years ago
and somehow still bone close, so yes, I know how to stand back up

I'm just not sure who I am standing up with anymore.
Where do I belong after I wrote myself as an outsider?

TRAGIC INTERVIEW

We will ask you if it is true
We will ask you how true it is
We will ask you where you're from
We will ask you to verify you belong
We will ask you about vice and god
We will ask you to legitimize blood
We will ask for a pathos worthy childhood
We will ask you about your thronged body
We will ask why you inhabit both and many
We will ask if your kin tolerates such veracity
We will ask if you've told the whole story
We will ask if you are attracted to danger
We will ask you if your shame overlingers
We will ask for trauma to be in past tense
We will ask you to narratively arc triumph
We will ask you to lip service progress
We will ask you about free speech
We will ask to contract your name
We will ask you to trouble in stereotypes
We will ask you stroke those fleshy ethics
We will ask how outsiders may write about you
We will ask you for your blanket endorsement
We will ask you wax widespread as hot and now
We will ask you attest to your own exceptionalism
We will ask to couch your fine ass in the theoretical

We will ask you to table round with your enemies

We will ask that you prove pain makes great art

We will ask you to represent en masse

We will ask you to do it for less

We will ask for your free consultation

We will ask you to recommend your own

We will ask where do you find the time

We will ask you to exalt your labour

We will ask if your success is a surprise

We will ask if you're surprised to be alive

We will ask you to front face as the hero

We will ask you exhibit the future possible

We will ask how the next gen will fathom and ken

We will ask for a kind offering to the institution

We will ask you for the ever positive spin

We will ask you cleave homage and imitation

We will ask your craft for credible dimension

We will ask if the work appears to be uneven

We will ask you to trial your live version

We will ask you how true it is

We will ask you if it is true

A police officer in the 1990s: Are you sure this really happened? You look fine. Shouldn't you be crying?

An audience member after nearly every literary event where I have read work from the first person experiential: Did all that really happen to you? And look at you now. You really turned your life around.

STREGHERIA INSTRUCTIONAL #2

shot of bourbon
a lit candle
a wooden match
a pinch of salt

Above: a list of ingredients for the drunken flame spell.

I'm making this shit up as I go.
Instructions below:

Sprinkle the bourbon with salt and pour a spoon's worth into your cupped left palm.
Take up the match with your right hand and light it off the candle's flame.

Kiss the firewater held in your left with the match head.

Your nervous system will say *no*
but the flame knows what to do.

You will see the spirit leap blue before you feel
its heat. Clap your hands together. You won't burn.

Notice how, this time, fear is not followed by consequence.
Notice how, this time, fear only wants to make itself seen.

DEAR INCORRECTNAME
FOUND AND REDACTED FROM MY INBOX

Please allow me to introduce myself as the **OfficialTitle** at the **College**_University_ GovernmentFunded**Institution**. At my **Institutional**PlaceOfEmployment we are Studying_**Othering**the**Living**HellOutof *Prostitution* in Canada_FeministViews on *Prostitution_Prostitution***Exploitation**Trafficking_and other topics related to your "hellish existence."

Your book *How Poetry Saved My Life* is on my students' critical book review list alongside TextsbyFeministsWho**Hate**You and Unethical**Researchers**. I feel strongly that your perspective would contribute to my students' learning. Sorry for the ridiculously late notice, but I want to invite you to visit our class next Friday. I do not have funds for guest speakers, but I would be happy to offer a $50 honorarium from my own **Salary**thatIsFourTimesWhatyouEarnedLastYear and parking permit for the day. Please let me know if this would work for you.

Dear IncorrectName

I am writing on behalf of the **Academic**ConferenceWithA\$200+**Fee**PerAttendee.
Part of this year's goal is to include a performance "cabaret" [erroneous use
of quotation marks for reasons unknown] that will feature any or all varieties
of literary performance (spoken word, performance poetry, slam poetry, sound
poetry, etc) with a focus on the voices of diverse populations.

Your presence at this "cabaret" would be of great value
to the conference attendees in their role as **Analytical**Onlookers.

I have heard back from the PlanningCommittee regarding finances and what we can
offer you is a Below**Standard**ArtistFee honorarium, but we are tight so__could you
accept a conference pass? We have several other authors who are only getting
conference passes. So paying you is a bit of a "double standard" [substantiated
use of quotation marks] and there might be hard feelings.

I look forward to hearing from you.

Dear IncorrectName

WeAreOtherArtists. We'd love if you would come to OurSHOW and read
your work_talk about your work_talk about your life_talk about the state of
our community_talk about doing work in community. No hard hitting talk_just
talk talk_casual talk. You would be fabulous. Our stage is yours
for one hour. We expect around 150 guests.

This is your opportunity to reach a large crowd.

We don't offer you an appearance fee, but you will see
OurVision is VeryInnovative.

Dear Amber Dawn

I am a Writer_Artist_BodyThatisHoldingStory.

I have always loved &admired your work &it would be an honour to have your feedback. It would be awesome if you could read my ScriptCollectionNovelOutlineTreatise &give me some honest &brutal feedback. Read it whenever you want! I hope I see you in person soon! I can come by your office. Do you still work at ArtsCommunityJob_ FrontLineSupport_DropIn_HeathCentre_**College**University?

I am HoldingaStory &it is PAINFUL. How did you   write your first book?

I have always wanted to be   a writer. Did it feel like a relief

                                                        to get that first book out?
How do you read in front of all those people   &do interviews   &does your mom

still speak to you?   I'm afraid of my parents
                                                &hometown   &readers
&MySurvivorsStory &what people will think   if I   SpeakMyTruth.

What do you like about being a writer?

TOUCH ≠ TOUCH SCREEN

"At what point do women realize they are not welcome in public places? The first time you feel a hand slip between your legs on the subway? ... Or is it later, when somebody ... calls you a bitch on Twitter ...?"

—Elizabeth Renzetti, from *Shrewed: A Wry and Closely Observed Look at the Lives of Women and Girls*

i.

I put it in ink: *I write*
for other survivors. I am listening.

As well, in ink, presently, on this page: *I'm here*
for the divine and complex work that is healing.

But how can I be a bright witness to survivorship
shown on a five inch liquid crystal display?

How do I go from touch

to touch screen?

ii.

You see
I came to disclosure
  and to poetry
present

meaning
in the room
a circle and a chain
pass the tissue box

and then in the street
a rally and a chain
banners lit with names
pass the vigil candles
in wax paper cups

meaning I stood
with grief, stood
and stand with grief
     I still
remember the faithful snag
of kin's calloused thumbs
because they touched me
hands clasped elbows strong-locked together
and sometimes mouths kissing in the streets
rough loving in the streets   sometimes

rough loving our grief is a kind of promise   aurora

    cockcrow ante meridiem a promise to let tomorrow in

skin on skin the soma of verse of song

of raising our whispers up to pitch

together

          this is how

      my healing took shape

          and this is how poetry

          held its vital language

          out to me

iii.

This is   we haven't met but I saw you   onstage   vulnerable   not sure what to say
a collage   read your memoir   in an emergency so brave shameless courageous
of select   my courage was stolen   my father   my first boyfriend I was sixteen it took
Twitter   me years   trance marijuana have you tried CBT   Hypnotherapy? trigger
messages   warning Percocet addiction   attached is a poem I wrote about rape   I live
from the   nearby you're in the V6A right? I made you a gift   be present with me
71 total   I don't want a support worker   my asshole doctor I'd rather talk to you
I have   I'm so sorry   must be soul destroying   your life   pretty much non stop
received   abuse the abuse the abuse the abuse abuse abuse   until I moved out
since I   what advice would you give me? his hands on me   his fist   your poetry
published   chronic pain depression PTSD dyspareunia vaginismus will it go away?
my memoir   I gave your book to my daughter   my sobriety circle   to my youth group
in which   only other survivors get it   we're superheroes   I have to keep believing
the sender   please come visit me at the hospital?   my own family thinks I'm crazy
discloses   I thought she/he/they loved me but   I struggle to leave my house at night
surviving   when I read your poetry I felt   I'm this close to giving up   end the pain
sexual   I think I'm stone too like you fuck like you   am like you   I was just
violence   a baby nothing but monsters we should meet IRL   I'm afraid every day

I know exactly where these disclosures would soft land on my body.
I know what words I would say, in real time, what assurances, what affinities.
I am here for the divine and complex work that is healing.   Except—

—except my body
my gritty affinities
my **R**hythm **H**elps **Y**our **T**ender **H**eart **M**ove
ritualized mnemonics my recovered wisdoms
honorifics   my bows
            and my downs
            right over left   arms locked
            at the elbows
            calls and responses
            tender skill share
            collective methods
            mutual understandings   all

            miscarry on social media.

I'm ashamed
to admit it

but my teeth and grace
bite mum in the volume.

Traumacasting is a new commune that has me
once more afraid of survivors' stories

after the brave spit I licked
after all that has been taught
sharply imparted   all that
I've learned   am learning
yet to learn
I am afraid
again

afraid of the pitiful
and public narrations
our bodies
are being
inscribed
into.

iv.

I could readily assemble a collage of messages
from senders who have called me a fucking whore
but that would be one knife-edged cut and paste job.

Although, perhaps, it should be said
that holding survivors' stories   and   meeting with hatred

on the same platform
straps disclosure and violence together in ways
                              that disservice healing.

Just survivors, I'm talking only to you now (literally you).
Did your abuse fever teach you to solder belonging and harm?
Were you seen and were you shamed in the same
original place? Did you inherit
a coercive dichotomy?
Anxious arousal hand
me downs?

Does your public network see you and hate you in looping rounds?
Does logging on harm you? Does all this somehow feel familiar?

v.

How do any of us go from touch

                    to touch screen?

                              And, mercy please, back to touch again?

                    IDK about you, but I really miss when bent queers used to fist
                                        each other to cope. Am I alone here?

                    I mean, what if we just quit the internet for a spell
                              and tried to duck bill back to our highest selves?

                                                  Speak to me, please.
                                                        I'm listening.

Speak—

ing of gape

one redeemable thing about Twitter
is that we can still post sphincter pics.

Hang with me. Hang in. This is not a digression.
Buttholes are a fundamental part of the conversation.

vi.

Instagram shadowbans live or cartoon anuses, genitals
and female-presenting or -assumed nipples.

                                        Shadowban—
meaning content made un discoverable
un sharable   un see able

and as of 2018, Instagram fully bans the soliciting
of sexual services and sexually explicit language.

In 2018, Facebook introduced its Sexual Solicitation Policy banning sex
chat, any mention of sex, sexual roles, preferences or sexualized body parts.

Tumblr—an e-mpire built on shared smut—safe-moded sex
from its e-xistence. This also in 2018.

Don't even get me started on Craigslist Personals
or Backpage, both shut down in 2018.
loudly crying face emoji skull & crossbones
emoji broken heart broken heart broken

                                        So what's up with 2018?

Maybe *what's up with 2018?* is best answered by going back to 1996?

In 1996 I turned low rent full service sex, right? Billed my hustle
in a forty-character ad in the back of the *Vancouver Buy and Sell*.
During those way back days, I took the bus to the suburbs
to place the ad in person. Indeed, I was one of many sex workers
whose ad revenue economically aroused weekly newspapers.
My whore lore predates social media.   IKR

FR   I'm saying 1996 is when internet legislation Section 230 first declared:
"No provider or user of an interactive computer service shall be treated
as the publisher or speaker of any information provided by another
information content provider."
                              Meaning that social media platforms shall allow
for user generated content without holding those platforms responsible
for whatever those users might post.

You get this? Sphincter pics belonged to and were the responsibility of said
sphincter pic poster. Our buttholes did not belong to, were not disseminated
and were not censored by Facebook   yet.

I began to hustle early chat forums. Eventually, web chat helped me get off
the streets. Some sex workers with access trailblazed their own networks.
Tech savvy whores had websites before public libraries did, before banks.

Wanna guess who else breathed life into the internet? Queers.
AOL was GayOL. PlanetOut predates Facebook by eight years.
Queers needed to find each other, see each other, love each other
learn from each other, safely, often anonymously.   IOW Queers
and whores, and our glorious buttholes, made social media.

                                                    Now we can talk about 2018.

Let's talk about 2018 when
FOSTA-SESTA (Fight Online Sex Trafficking Act and Stop
Enabling Sex Traffickers Act) was passed as law by US Congress
on April 11, marking the first ever exception to Section 230.

So after twenty-two years, yes, twenty-two years, social media platforms
where made responsible for user generated content if that content may be
intended for sex work yes
                        all sex work, yes, consensual sex work and, yes
anything like a butthole or a female-presenting-assumed nipple, and yes
            responsible for or in authority of images, words and phrases
                that mend desire together
                with age, race, size, orientation, disability, labour
                economics and any bodies subject to other-ness.

And with other-ness, I'm talking about
fat babes in neon green lingerie, about two brown men
kissing, about trans women being radiant and using
their real fucking names. I'm talking about
masculine-presenting-assumed folk with baby bumps. I'm talking sexual
assault survivors showing off the scars on our inner thighs. I'm talking about
women posting screenshots of the violent Tinder messages we receive
every damn day. I'm talking about
speaking up. I'm talking language
reclamation. I'm talking decolonizing
sexualities. I'm talking gagged faggots
about dyke march photos
torn down. I'm talking
about locked accounts.

I'm talking about the systemic erasure of #blackqueermagic #youOKsis
#whiteterrorism #EveryBodyIsBeautyful #breastfeeding #psoriasislife
#girlswithhairyarmpits #FeministTinder #curvygirls #everybodyisbeautiful
#lesbiansofinstagram #decolonizingbeauty #gayasian
#boysintights #latinasdoitbetter #gaykiss
#twink #kink #teamthick #samelove

Yes, correct, the internet was wholly changed in 2018
because the US Congress hates sex workers, which by the way
means they hate you too (literally you).

vii.

If anyone here is veering into *but what about the commodification of bodies, what about the male gaze* or such lines of inquiry—I can't.

I can't ask this poem to deconstruct "hate the sin, love the sinner" nonsense. I can't ask this poem to make anyone unpack notions of *good* sexuality versus *taboo* sexuality much less invisibilized bodies or criminalized bodies.

I can't ask this poem to verify the connection between whorephobia and wealth concentration, nationalism, white supremacy and religious conservatism. A poem is always a mirror that we must hold up before us but catch that education elsewhere.

viii.

I'm talking about this—
power holding backlash.   How dare we get those likes
                          those shares, take up virtual space

                          speak truths, share strategy, love our ash and phoenix
                          bodies, rise up or dig deep, whichever way or all
                          directions at once.

                                    We can be nimble AF
                                    but how dare we?

Make the internet
white relentlessly white again
str8 cis thin and norm again
Redesign the sightline
of hating women.   I'm talking about this
                      power holding backlash.

                                              I think about this a lot—

                                              what it means to spend upwards
                                                    of two hours per day
                                                    on platforms that believe
                                              we should not legally exist
                                                    un   see   able

ix.

> I ask myself if we are permitted
> to visibly exist online at all
> solely to be blamable
> rape-able
> hate
> -able

Social media platforms are still
not responsible for hate speech.

This angle of Section 230 remains cocked, permissible hashtags include:
#penisparty #fucklgbt #fuckfeminism #fuckwomen #LiesToldByFemales
#IHateFemalesWho #gunsofinstagram #whitegenocide #nazi #milktwitter #maga #kek

Make the internet
a hateful megacosm again.

x.

In this poem, I am trying to justify
that logging on harms me.

In every corner, everywhere
there is a survivor being made
to justify the harms
being done to them.

In this poem, I had also hoped to write about shitposters.
Shitposters—meaning online users trolling for the sake of trolling.

And incels—
a portmanteau of involuntary celibates.
who believe women methodically withhold sex and believe
that violence against sexually active women is an appropriate response.

And I had hoped
to write about the rising online currency of MGTOW
MGTOW—an acronym for Men Going Their Own Way
Cishet male separatists, ideological celibates, anti-
feminist, who believe so-called (binary) gender equality
has collapsed their once-great civilization.

When MGTOWs hire

sex workers they claim it doesn't count.

You don't pay them for sex, you pay them to leave

is a popular phrase used in this rising online community.

MGTOW posts aren't shadowbanned.

                                   I see these posts all the time.

Money is attached to sex workers disappearing, but it's
not sex workers who profit from this departure.

Tell me, who is being *consumed*?

MGTOWs have sent me threatening messages, alongside the messages
from women who have disclosed sexual violence to me. I don't know
how to respond
to this mind fuck
of a division
within my DMs.

This poem is me
responding.

xi.

In this poem, I wanted to confess that I am captured by the comments
and comments and comments and comments, in particular by comments
that suggest violent men, even latent mass murders, should hire sex workers.

I see women post these comments.
I see women only once removed, friends of friends, post.
I see friends of friends, self-identified feminists comment
on how sex workers should cede ourselves as rape-able.
I see followers post on how sex workers should swallow
this violence.

I see friends, followers who have read my memoir
like these comments and comments and I am captured.

This is far more complex than logging off.
I confess, I never log off.   I am captured.

xii.

I'm an artist, a queer woman artist who's written about trauma.
Social media presence is expected of me, being public
and being hated, is just part of the job, right?
Occupational hazard. Professional dues.

      If we are going to be made to pay—then let's keep flipping
      the figurative billfold of our beautiful other-ness. Can we
      make each other that promise? Let us
      be the buttholes we want to see in that world.
                      Let us search for each other
      online and in the streets and, mercy please, in verse. Let us
      want for something greater than anxious arousal.   Let us
      testify to this desire, record and share
      what we've learned about healing
      what we are learning
      about being present
      about being.

We already know we are hated, yeah yeah. We
already know which lines and character spaces are torn down.

But power holding backlashers don't know
after all this time, after my blood spit and ejaculate and after yours
after our rage that shifts the transmission, after a grief that realigns eternity
after our cultural content is made on trend then erased again, after everything
made is remade and remade and remembered and revered, after all
power holders still don't know
that we will never be un discoverable
un sharable   un see able

I put it in ink: *I'm here*
for the divine and complex work that is healing.

This is how my healing took shape

and this is how poetry
might yet hold its vital language out to us.

THE RINGING BELL

Lately I've been reexamining what it means to write poetry. The thing is I
grew suspicious of the page after I published a memoir, a memoir about poetry
(and about backwoods hookups   bad dates cocaine forty dollar blow jobs
four chord guitar Gucci belt buckles   birthrighting into madness loving
my butch wife my chosen family moon cycles   habit forming medication
Parisian lesbians screech owls   second hand leather   two hundred and fifty
dollar blow jobs   and more blow jobs and more poetry).

Whatever is written becomes beautifully suspended.
Have I transcended or have I stayed my own trauma?

I once read reprinted lines of my poetry on an arts council funded
public transportation banner, while taking the bus to my doctor's
office to ask for a prescription sleeping pill refill.

I used to liken a poem to praying. Is that right?
Not the woo and gratitude praying served by queer witches.
Childhood praying. As a girl I genuflected to the tabernacle
and insisted on sitting next to the stained glass window.
On the right kind of Sunday sun would send a slice of pink
light through the glass and down to the porcelain tile floor.
If I reached my hand out, pink light made my fingers glow.
Hand bells rang as padre said *hoc est enim corpus meum.*

                                                          this is my body

I was baptized at four years old, quite late for roman rite. My ma wanted
me to accept god, to be old enough to say it aloud, to initiate myself.

At four, I was old enough to say *yes*
yes, I receive the light of christ and old enough
to recognize water, candle and cross as reoccurring
symbols, but, developmentally, faith was impossible.
Preschoolers lack an understanding of abstract thought.

In place of abstraction, four year olds are animists.
Everything is alive and has a purpose. Everything
feels and communicates. Nothing is inanimate.

What a marvellous
literally marvellous
stage in cognition.

So then, let's say my four year old self gave the bell
a human tongue, and the bell said *never mind your bent knee.*
Never mind the padre. The cross, the book, the mass, never mind.

And the bell said *hoc est enim corpus meum means*
this is my body, *but never mind*   this is my body
because you, child, will spend a lifetime
wondering if you will ever claim your own body
and wondering if poetry can help you make this claim.

                    I once read lines of my poetry quoted in the copy of a queer personal ad.
                    I can only hope the placer of said ad has her desires met and met again.

You see, I should be too old for mawkish longing, but still I want
to write the poem that returns me to the circle of Canadian tuxedo
or bras-as-outerwear dressed queers. All of us whisky licked or coming
up on MDMA. It was the '90s.
Spin-the-bottle parties were back in fashion.

Each time the bottle stopped a new couple performed
their derelict desire. *Tongue?* was a straightforward question
so was *chokehold?*

My spin paired me with a wiry butch who asked permission to be *rough?*
> *Rough* I agreed.
> *Spit?*
> *Yes. Spit.*
> We yanked one another around by the hair, licking, drooling. Later
we took our make out session to a warehouse loading zone a few blocks
from the party. Our voices yelped and echoed down the industrial alleyway.

I thought about how my expressions of pain were heavily moderated
as a child. Mine was a *don't make a sound, or else* kind of abuse.

Don't think about violence Don't think about violence
Don't think about violence Don't think about violence
Don't think about violence Don't think about violence   this is my body
Don't think about violence Don't think about violence   this is my body
                                                                          this is my body
                                                                          this is my body

Don't think about violence, I scolded myself as the wiry butch dropped
his pants. I fucked him in the open night air with both hands.
The way his pitch changed each time
he said *mmm hmmm baby* was astonishing.
He hooked into my underwear.
You next. Let me—

        No

        No?

I couldn't get to where wiry butch was going.
I was twenty two
and I hadn't yet google searched the shit out of PTSD.

I hadn't read studies that connect
the physiological and cognitive symptoms
of trauma to the nervous system   or to orgasm.
What I knew then was that cumming made me sick.

But I wanted more.
I wanted more than nausea and uncertainty. I wanted
to be worshipped on a courageous femme orgasmic altar.

Sacredness is a series of small acts
Sacredness is a series of small acts
Sacredness is a series of small acts
Sacredness is a series of small acts   this is my body
Sacredness is a series of small acts   this is my body
                                                             this is my body
                                                             this is my body
                                                             this is my body

Sacredness is a series of small acts. I told him *just a thumb knuckle.*
Just run your thumb knuckle over my clit a couple times. That's all.
That I can take.

I miss the two way mirror at the massage parlour off of Highway 91
where I worked for the better part of my twenties. I liked watching

the men wait. Seated neatly in the leather armchair, or pacing the length
of the lobby, or snagging a peppermint from the swan shaped candy bowl.

I liked to think of them as living curios on the other side of the glass.
Some would brush invisible debris from their buttoned shirts or beards

staring at themselves in the reflective side, unaware, or very much aware
of being watched by us girls (and that's what we always called ourselves—girls)

If one of us recognized the client, she slipped into easy shorthand: *two bill tipper*
sensual man drunk dick aggro wants GFE BBBJ big talker harmless harmless

> *harmless harmless*
> *that man is harmless*
> *looks rough*
> *but he's harmless*
> *harmless harmless*

I want poetry that makes me feel like I am
back on the viewing side of that two way mirror.

When the only clock in the room has stopped ticking, is it poetry?

When dust adopts the only framed photograph of your lost beloved, is it poetry?
I believe it is poetry, yes, that asks me to remember her however I can.

Tell me, because I really can't figure this out on my own, is poetry
like standing in the gravel road in the dried up bankrupt town
where I was born watching a thunderstorm roll in?

The neighbours all gathered on this same gravel road to watch the same storm.
The only other times I remember the neighbours gathered together like that
was to gawk at the cop cars parked in our driveway.
I used to own these memories as shame.
I believed the neighbours hated us.

Except the neighbours never used the word *hate*.
The word *hate* is an antagonism I assigned to this memory, and why
would I let memory be used like that? Why would *hate* appear in a poem?

Yes, my neck knows cower and loll like hate is expected. Leave it
to a Great Lake thunderstorm to tilt my head up. The heat wave
had gone on too long. We waited for rain. We looked up. Thunderclap.
Electricity. Swollen clouds. Neighbours gathered.
We looked up and looked up.

I once found reprinted lines of my poetry in an academic journal that used the words "textualities" "métissage" and "polyphonic" in the essay title alone —and people tell me they don't *get* poetry.

I wouldn't mind if my poetry mimicked racing tipsy down the subway stairs in platform heels to barely catch the last train of the night. The other drunks nodding a wordless celebration that we will all make it home before dawn.

I want poetry like Yma Sumac or Freddie Mercury hitting those high notes. What in goddess's name is it like to have a five octave range?

Lately my poetry seems to tempt brush fire.
I was fourteen when we lit the field on fire.

The landlord said that if we could work
the clay heavy soil we could plant a garden.

I had been molested in that field and inside
the timber frame house and inside a trailer

abandoned at the end of the dirt driveway.
But it was the time in the field I thought about

as smoke rose from the tufty tops of milk thistle.
We burned a half acre of scrub. Burnt stilt grass.

Burnt horsemint. Burnt Queen Anne's lace. Burnt buckthorn.
Burnt balsam. Burnt ground clover. Burnt glory vine.

My job was to stand guard before the tree line
water buckets ready to drench any flame that spread too far. The field
       became humble ash and I didn't want to wash the smell
       of smoke
              from my hair for weeks.

this is my body

Unlike a hangover or a bruise
poetry gives no fucks about corporeal or temporal boundaries.
When I read this poem aloud I can still smell smoke in my hair.

this is my body

Read every poem by Joy Harjo and Sapphire and Sharon Olds
one careful line at a time. Then read
every poem backward
last line to first to find
what meaning is hidden
outside of chronology.

Yeah uhm, you know that feeling when a preposterously gorgeous stranger asks you
to light her cigarette? Like when a preposterously gorgeous stranger sits beside you
at a book launch? Like when a preposterously gorgeous stranger recognizes you
as femme at first glance? Tell me how to write poetry that feels like that.

By writing this poem I acknowledge the blessing and privilege it is
that I am able to account for these very moments of my life.
I still believe poetry is a promise to never stop looking.
Look up and look up.

The field keeps coming up
in poetry and in dreams. Same difference.

I think about how that half acre of land might perform on the page.
Not balefire and ash. Let me show you the harvest.

The landlord told us the clay heavy soil was no good
and there are few things I love more than when landlords are wrong.

A garden grew well into October. I could no longer pinpoint the spot
where I had been molested, only that the earth was abundant.

Canned tomatoes rimmed our kitchen floor. Basil hung from the ceiling.
There was so much zucchini my ma couldn't give it away.

I remember sitting at the picnic table snapping bush beans. Maybe
we did or maybe we didn't remember the *idioma* for green thumb.

I mani verdi. Pollice verdi. Come si dice
we have the gift of growing food from soot?

Come si dice we are well fed because we lit it all on fire?
Come si dice there is always something on the other side of fire?

Once I saw a line of my poetry written on a protest
sign at a dyke march.
Now is as good a time as any to admit that I hoped
poetry would carry me.

Is it too late for me
to believe in being
uplifted?

Is it too late for me
to make grand statements about poetry?

And the wraithy hiss that often visits jaw and ear is poetry. this is my body
And the gritty hymns that enchant mending skins are poetry. this is my body
And every callous earned by heel and by thumb are poetry. this is my body
And the sharp plummet of another nightmare is poetry.
The feral shade of blue that shows itself at four a.m. is poetry

When only maw and gut can hold some memories, it is poetry.
If it's not yet, or not ever, on the page or tongue, it is still poetry.

And the ringing bell said *hoc est enim corpus meum*
means this is my body.
this is my body
this is my body

And how will I claim my body this time?
And will poetry still help me make this claim?

ACKNOWLEDGMENTS

My Art Is Killing Me and Other Poems marks my eighth book with Arsenal Pulp Press. I hold these relationships in the highest esteem, and my dearest thanks goes to Publisher Brian Lam, Associate Publisher Robert Ballantyne, Marketing Director Cynara Geissler, Editor Shirarose Wilensky, Editorial and Marketing Assistant Jaiden Dembo and, the newest team member, Production Manager Jaz Welch.

Thank you to Sachiko Murakami for editorial guidance, and for being an all-around poem genius.

For engaging in critical and often loving conversation with me, I thank Jillian Christmas, Doretta Lau, Nancy Lee, Emily Pohl-Weary, Kevin Chong, Sara Graefe, Catherine Hernandez, Carrianne Leung, Dina Del Bucchia, Jen Sookfong Lee, Lindsay Wong, Lisa Jean Helps, Casey Plett, Eden Robinson, Cherie Dimaline, Chelene Knight, Larissa Lai, Kai Cheng Thom, Adèle Barclay, Yilin Wang, Meghan Bell, Juliane Okot Bitek jaye simpson, SJ Sindu and Carleigh Baker.

I am grateful for my decade-long marriage to CJ Rowe. Learning all that love holds is my greatest creative pursuit.

And finally, undying thanks (and fandom) to artist Jaik Puppyteeth for re-envisioning works from his *Death* series for the cover and interior artwork.

Photo credit: Sarah Race

AMBER DAWN is the author of the novels *Sodom Road Exit* (2018) and *Sub Rosa* (winner of a Lambda Literary Award, 2010), the Vancouver Book Award–winning memoir *How Poetry Saved My Life* (2013), and the Dorothy Livesay Poetry Prize–nominated collection *Where the words end and my body begins* (2015). She is also the editor of *Fist of the Spider Woman: Tales of Fear and Queer Desire* and the co-editor of *With a Rough Tongue: Femmes Write Porn* and *Hustling Verse: An Anthology of Sex Workers' Poetry*. She teaches creative writing at Douglas College in Vancouver and leads several low-barrier community writing classes.